Illustrations: John Dillow (Beehive Illustration)

Photos: 123RF Limited · DigitalVision · EyeWire

Author: Geneviève De Becker

English Translation: Sally-Ann Hopwood (Prolingua)

English Edited Edition: Eurolina Inc.

Graphical Design: Cécile Marbehant

ANIMALS FOUND ON THE FARM

THE COW

The cow eats grass from the meadow. It must chew the grass for a long time before being able to digest it. The cow is a grazing animal. It is a ruminant, which means it is a cud-chewing mammal. When kept in a barn the farmer feeds the cow hay, cereal and corn.

The cow produces milk that is collected by the farmer who milks the cow by pulling on its 4 udders. The milk is used to make cheese, fresh cream or yogurt.

The baby cow called a calf is born after a 9 month gestation period, and feeds on milk from its mother's udders.
A male calf is called a bull and a female calf is called a heifer.

THE DUCK

The female duck lays eggs from which little ducklings covered in yellow or brown down feathers hatch. On their first day, the ducklings follow their mother for a swim. With a watchful eye, the mother duck checks that her little ducklings are following her.

The mallard duck is the ancestor of most domestic ducks, such as the white farm duck. The male mallard duck is recognized by his colorful feathers, while the female duck has brown feathers that serve as camouflage.

The wild duck is most often found on lakes or ponds where it finds its best food supply. Frogs, mollusks and small fish are caught by plunging their head in the water.

8

SHEEP

Sheep live in flocks. The male sheep called the ram is recognized by its horns, which it uses to fight. A female sheep is called a ewe. Female sheep are more numerous and are often accompanied by their young. A baby sheep is called a lamb.

In the mountains, shepherds take their flock of sheep to pastures so that they can graze on the grass.
In the pasture you can hear the bleating sounds of the sheep.

Once a year, the farmer shaves the sheep for their wool with the help of electric shears. This task is done in less than 3 minutes. The milk of sheep is tasty to drink and it can also be used to make cheese.

THE GOOSE

The white goose is a domesticated animal that is often found on a farm. Geese are raised for their eggs, meat and their livers.

Geese are noisy and loud. They scream, hiss and honk. This animal is as protective of its territory as a guard dog. It will protect its territory with loud cries and will even attack intruders.

The male goose called the gander, and the female goose form a couple for life. They raise and defend their young goslings together.

THE HEN

Like all birds, the hen lays eggs. The eggs can be cooked and eaten soft boiled, fried, scrambled or hardboiled. After 21 days of a hen sitting on her eggs, cute little chicks hatch.

The male hen called the rooster lives with several hens in a henhouse. The rooster is recognized by its bright red chest and colorful feathers. It is the rooster that sometimes wakes you up early in the morning with its unique cry of "cock-a-doodle-doo".

The hen eats earthworms, insects and grains of corn. It swallows gravel that helps it to grind and digest the grains it has eaten.

THE RABBIT

The rabbit has two large ears and legs that are perfect for hopping. It has a very keen sense of smell that can be seen with the twitching of its nose.

In the wild, rabbits live in burrows in which the female rabbit called the doe gives birth to 2 to 7 baby rabbits, after only a gestation period of 1 month. Rabbits can have 4 or 5 litters a year.

Rabbits eat grass, roots, leaves and bark.
A large colony of rabbits can destroy a farmer's entire harvest.

THE HORSE

The horse eats grass that it shreds with the aid of its incisors and then chews with its molars. There are several breeds of horses, including the work horse that can pull carts and plows.

Horseback riding is a greatly loved sport. A special bond exists between horse and trainer, once trust is established. More than just a loyal friend, a horse requires daily care.

The foal or filly is born after an 11 month gestation period, and can already stand up within half an hour of birth. It nurses from its mother until the age of 6 months and starts eating grass after 1 month.

THE GOAT

The female goat called the nanny and the male goat called the billy goat eat all the plants that they come across, as well as almost anything else, including paper and clothes.

A young goat called a kid is born after a 5 month gestation period, and feeds on its mother's milk until the age of 6 weeks.

The goat is a favourite farm animal for children. It is calm and fun to pet. You can drink goat's milk or use it to make delicious cheeses. The wool of a goat is used to make carpets or for knitting.